C000255671

How Sai Baba Attracts
Without Direct Contact

Diary of a 21st Century Sai Devotee

Dr. Tommy S. W. Wong

Dedicated to

my parents, Wong Sze Fong and Woo En Yueh

my parents-in-law, Sum Chip Shing and Ko Luk Ying

my darling wife, Christina

and my wonderful sons, Alston, Lester and Hanson

Acknowledgement

I like to thank Bhagavan Sri Sathya Sai Baba for selecting me as his instrument in authoring this book for the benefit of mankind. I also like to thank him for the many blessings he has showered on me, including the spiritual and worldly experiences that transformed me into a more humane being and a more enlightened soul.

Preface

On 20 October 1940, Bhagavan Sri Sathya Sai Baba announced "*I no longer belong to you. Maya (delusion) has left me. My devotees are eagerly calling me.*" Since then, tens of millions of people around the world have been attracted to him and become his devotees. For those who have become devotees in the earlier years (pre-21st century), many of them enjoyed direct physical contact with Baba, such as touching (sparshan) and conversations (sambhashan). Through personal experiences, they also enjoyed the commonly known attractions of Baba such as materialization of physical objects, instant healing of illnesses, speedy recovery of financial problems, and realization of personal desires. Through such direct contacts and personal experiences, they have become devout Sai devotees and have firm faith in Baba.

On the other hand, for those who have become devotees in the later years (during 21st century), the chances of having such direct contacts with Baba are very slim. So, how can these devotees secure firm faith in Baba? In this book, I share my experiences in which they show that Baba actually offers other types of attractions without the need for direct physical contact. These attractions have enabled me to secure firm faith in Baba, to become a more humane being and a more enlightened soul. Through my devotion, I have also gained insights on how to become a master of life. May this sharing be beneficial to you.

Om Sai Ram!

Tommy S. W. Wong
Singapore
September 2009

Table of Contents

Chapter 1

Early years

I was born in Hong Kong in 1952. For my primary and secondary education, I attended two Christian schools (1959-67) in Hong Kong and one Catholic school (1967-69) in England. Despite these early influences, religion had little or no impact on me. Even during my adulthood when I attended many more talks of different faiths, I still did not find the teachings or people within those groups appealing enough for me to join them. I was truly an atheist and used to ridicule people of faiths. So, it was most curious that even well before I became a Sai devotee, I was very interested in Sai Baba and other spiritual gurus. In those days, when I met a Sai devotee or someone who has some experiences of Baba, I would go to great lengths to find out what he knew about Baba or details of his experiences. I would also read books on Baba and found his teachings and miracles most appealing. Although I was not a Sai devotee in those early years, undoubtedly Baba was drawing me to him. Four notable incidents happened.

In 1985, my wife Christina and I migrated from Hong Kong to Singapore, where I joined a civil engineering department as an academic. Through work, I got to know some of the academics in the other university in Singapore which also had a civil engineering department. One of these academics was a long-time, devout Sai devotee (Brother Selvalingam). Since there were only two universities in Singapore with civil engineering department, and Brother Selvalingam's area of specialization was exactly the same as mine, we were supposed to be bitter rivals. In any case in 1993, as I was due to go to England for my 8-month sabbatical leave, and Brother Selvalingam was due to leave Singapore and migrate to Australia, I invited him to dinner. Although he did not join us for dinner, he nevertheless came and brought me a Sai book. See how Baba worked. Of all the people in Singapore, Baba sent my rival to send me the book entitled "*Man of Miracles*" by Howard Murphet. I read the book some years later, and it moved me closer to the "light". So, it was my rival who put me on to the path to God. How extraordinary? Undoubtedly, Brother Selvalingam was putting Baba's teachings into practice (i.e. "*Love All, Serve All*" and "*Help Ever, Hurt Never*" even to your rival). I am forever grateful to him for his divine gift, and I still have the book today. In 1999, when I attended a conference in Australia, I made the extra effort of flying from Sydney to Melbourne to see Brother Selvalingam. See how Baba shows us how to behave!

The second incident happened in 1992, completely unplanned and unknowing, I stumbled into a mind control seminar in which they taught the alpha meditation. As part of the seminar, the instructor talked about Sai Baba and promoted vegetarianism. This seminar actually opened my door to spirituality, and to the instructor I am forever grateful. Through the seminar, I was converted to a vegetarian. Now I could see that it was all Baba's plan and attending the seminar was no coincidence. By changing to the "right" diet, it was much easier for me to become a Sai devotee and visit Baba later. See how Baba prepares us!

The third incident happened after I returned to Singapore from my sabbatical leave in England. From time to time since 1980, I would write letters to newspapers or magazines voicing my opinions. On 12 June 1998, Asiaweek magazine (which ceased operation in 2001) published a special issue on "Freedom" which contained many articles on how the "local" leaders have successfully overthrown their "foreign" counterparts. The success was attributed to the ethnicity-based or religion-based nationalism. For some inexplicable reason even though I was not yet a Sai devotee, I responded to these articles with a letter quoting the following Baba saying:

> *"In this world, there is only one race and that is the human race, and there is only one religion and that is the religion of love."*

I also suggested that we should see the world from this perspective which was a better basis to achieve world harmony and true freedom. The letter was published on 17 July 1998. See how Baba influences us!

The fourth incident happened subsequent to the 1992 mind control seminar. During the seminar, I learned how to make connection with God through meditation. Baba is of course God in human form (avatar). Since then, by analyzing life events up to that time, I sensed that my life mission was to conduct research within a specialized topic in civil engineering. However, I had my doubts. One day in 1995, I asked Baba to give me a sign if my life mission was indeed to conduct research within this specialized topic. He gave me the following sign.

As an academic in a civil engineering department in Singapore, I would publish papers in journals and conferences, and in 1992, I also published one book. With the papers published in international journals, as a result of the worldwide circulation, I would from time to time receive requests for copies of my papers. These requests were usually made in standard forms, post cards or by emails. On the other hand, my book being published by a local publisher had a very limited circulation. Hence, I did not expect and have had no request for copies of my book. As such, I was flabbergasted to receive a very neat hand written letter requesting for a copy of my book by a professor in New Jersey, USA. And to add to this extraordinary incident, this happened just one day after I made the request to Baba.

Subsequent to the above sign, I conducted my research with renewed vigor. In the course of my work, I noticed that there was a common misconception in a design procedure, and this misconception had persisted for decades. For the sake of my profession, I wanted to write an article to clarify this concept. While I made a start on the article, I found it difficult to complete it. Further, I was looking for a meaningful foreword so that the readers could recognize the focus of the article instantly. The article was suspended until April 2001 when I came across the following saying by Baba in John Hislop's book entitled *"Conversation with Bhagavan Sri Sathya Sai Baba"*:

> *"Lack of understanding is not too dangerous. Misunderstanding is very dangerous."*

Inspired by the saying, I impulsively went back to my office that Sunday evening and completed the article. This happening was quite extraordinary because the chances for me to go to the office on a Sunday evening were practically zero. Further, an article of this nature usually takes many days or even weeks to complete. For this article, it took an incredible period of one evening. After completing the article, it was submitted to an international journal which was duly accepted for publication in September 2001.

Further happenings followed after the article was accepted. Usually, an accepted article only gets published after a minimum of six months after acceptance. So, I was astounded when I received an email in October 2001 informing me that the article was scheduled to be published in January 2002 – a mere four months after acceptance. This was unheard of in the world of journal publication. The January publication date had another significance. For articles published in January, it could appear on the first page of the journal. As there were many high quality articles ready to be published, for an article to appear on the first page was indeed an honor. My article appeared on the first page. Undoubtedly, all these were made possible because of Baba's grace. See how Baba inspires us!

These incidents showed me that even during those early years; Baba was already in my life. So, it was not surprising that in later years, I became a Sai devotee.

Chapter 2

Becoming a devotee

My wife and I are blessed with three sons – Alston was born in 1988, Lester in 1990 and Hanson in 1993. As part of their primary and secondary education, we used to send them to classes at a tuition center. In 2003, it was Hanson's turn to attend a tuition class every Friday from 7:30-9:30 pm. I used to send him to the tuition center which was situated in a shopping mall, and I would spent time there until Hanson finished his tuition. As I was getting more interested in Baba, I heard something called bhajan but completely did not know what it was. Subsequently, I found out that bhajan means devotional singing. In those days, I would also visit the main Sai Center in Singapore at Moulmein Road but only during daytime to do some prayer. One day it suddenly dawned on me that the Sai Center was only a 10-minute walk from the shopping mall and there were bhajan sessions on Friday evenings from 8-9 pm. I thought instead of hanging around at the shopping mall, why not go and take a look at what happens at a bhajan session. See how Baba arranged everything – both the location and timing were perfect for me to attend bhajan.

On 1 August 2003, I attended my first bhajan session. On that day, I entered the prayer hall completely not knowing anybody and not knowing what to expect. At the back of my mind, I did not expect too much as I usually found "religious" gatherings unappealing. In the past, as a norm, I would attend a gathering once and would not go again. Anyway, on this occasion, after I entered the hall, I first sat on the floor like other devotees. Then I felt uneasy, so I moved and sat on a chair at the back of the hall. Even this move was no coincidence. Shortly afterwards, a devotee (Brother Patrick) came in and sat next to me. He enquired whether I was a newcomer. As it turned out, Brother Patrick had the duty of sitting at the back of the hall and looked out for newcomers so that he would give some guidance. So, he explained to me the proceedings of the bhajan session, how to find the songs in the song book, and introduced to me the Chairman of the group (Brother Ho). All these guidance were important because I could then follow the session quite well. If not for his guidance, I would be lost and most probably, would not go again. For many times in my life, I found that Baba would send the right person at the right time when I needed help. After rendering help, the helper may then disappear from my life. On this occasion, Brother Patrick was such a person. Later, I found out that he actually did not attend bhajans regularly, and he only happened to be there that week. A couple of years later, he also left the group altogether.

Another significance of Friday bhajans was that they were in English. As I am English trained, I felt more at home with English bhajans as compared to Sanskrit or even Chinese bhajans. So, it was no coincidence that my first bhajan session was in English. After the first session, I felt quite good. So, I went back the following week, and then the following week. In fact, I have been going there practically non-stop every week for the next five years. In addition, I also attended bhajans on other days and at other centers. This was of course diametrically opposite to my normal reaction to "religious" gatherings, which showed me how much influence Baba had on me.

One thing I found by attending bhajans was that I felt bliss (atmananda), which was different from happiness. While happiness is a joy derived from some external events, bliss is inner joy and is derived from communion with God. When we install God into our hearts, we feel bliss. From many spiritual books I read, all the enlightened masters mentioned this feeling of bliss. I had never felt bliss prior to attending bhajans, and I had been searching for it for more than a decade. At long last,

I found it with Baba, and this is one of the biggest attractions of Baba. This feeling of bliss is intoxicating, and far greater than any happiness. Once you have tasted bliss, you will not want to slave for happiness. Indeed, this is the way to overcome materialism, for with all the materialistic things in the world, you may not gain bliss. On the other hand, by living with minimal materialism, you may live in bliss! Image what the world will be like if everyone lives with minimal materialism. Indeed, in Baba's discourse on 19 January 1983 entitled "*Ceiling on Desires – 1*", he said:

> "*Man needs some essential commodities for his sustenance and he should not aspire for more. We can learn a lesson in this respect from Nature. Only if air is available in sufficient quantity will it be comfortable and good. If it is excessive and there is a gale you will feel uncomfortable. When you are thirsty; you can consume only a limited quantity of water. You can't consume the entire water of the Ganga! We take only as much as is needed for the sustenance of the body.*"

Sure enough, I actually experienced minimal materialism during my first trip to see Baba.

Another thing happened after I attended bhajans. During that period, I faced a lot of difficulties at my place of work. In fact, I find that once you embarked on the spiritual path, you can expect a lot of difficulties because this is how we grow. In Baba's discourse on 1 June 1991 entitled *"Face the Challenges of Life"*, he said:

> *"Life is full of trials. If these difficulties are not there, life will have little value."*

So we should not consider difficulties as "bad" experiences. Instead, we should consider them as "good-bad" experiences that are "bad" experiences made to good use, as elaborated in Appendix A.

Although I was on the spiritual path, I had not reached the level where I could see all these worldly activities as maya (delusion) and not be affected by them. In fact, I was badly affected. During those days, it appeared to me that one bhajan was sung more often than others. Through this bhajan, I felt that Baba heard my anguish and gave me advice accordingly. See Baba can give advice through a bhajan. The bhajan is entitled *"Sing His Name"*:

*"When dark clouds fill your skies,
hiding sunshine from your eyes, sing
His Name, see His Form, hold on
O Lord, Sai Ram, sing His Name, see
His Form, hold on*

*When things are getting rough, and you
feel enough's enough, sing His Name,
see His Form, hold on
O Lord, Sai Ram, sing His Name, see
His Form, hold on*

*When life seems so unfair and no one
seems to care, sing His Name, see His
Form, hold on
O Lord, Sai Ram, sing His Name, see
His Form, hold on*

*Give a smile and say I can, come and
serve your fellowmen, sing His Name,
see His Form, hold on
O Lord, Sai Ram, sing His Name, see
His Form, hold on"*

I indeed held on and stayed on at the university
thereafter. Looking back I could see why Baba
advised me to stay. During subsequent years, I
enjoyed so much academic successes.

Since my first bhajan session in 2003, I became
more involved with the Friday group. In addition to

14

bhajans, my wife and I joined them in a Sai seva (volunteer service) in April 2004. In early 2005, Brother Ho invited me to read out Baba's message at the end of bhajan session. I readily accepted and did it several times. By this time, I would say that I have become a Sai devotee.

How Sai Baba attracts without direct contact

Chapter 3

First visit

Ever since I heard of Sai Baba and well before I became a devotee, I was interested to go to see him. Even with my regular attendance of bhajans at the Center, I still found it difficult to find someone who was willing to bring me. Although there were devotees who would bring big groups to see Baba, I refrained from joining them because of my health (enlarged prostate) problem, which caused me to go to toilet frequently. This was the physical explanation why I had not seen Baba yet. On the spiritual plane, the explanation was that Baba had not willed me to see him yet.

In any case, one day in 2005, I asked Brother Ho whether he knew anyone who was going to see Baba and was willing to bring me. I did not really expect a positive answer. So out of the blue and during a public Sai lecture at the Singapore Polytechnic on 11 May 2005, Brother Ho told me that Brother Ananda was going to see Baba and he was willing to bring me. When I heard this news, I could not believe it. Was it true that after such a long wait, I really had a chance to see Baba? I was so unsure that the news was real; I was even hesitant to tell my wife. Hours later after the news sunk in, I asked, "Who is this Brother Ananda?" I did not even know him. Anyway on the next day, I called him and found out he was going to Whitefield for the Buddha Purnima festival and he was only traveling with his wife. The advantage of going to Whitefield instead of Puttaparthi was that it did not have a long 3-hour drive, which would be a concern because of my health condition. So the arrangement was perfect, we were going to Whitefield and in a very small group. I then also found out his travel agent and his travel arrangement. I contacted this travel agent and made my own booking. In fact, there was just sufficient time for me to apply for the visa and get the air ticket for the departure to Bangalore on 18 May 2005. There was not a day to spare. See the perfection in Baba's calling.

Prior to departure date, I suggested to Brother Ananda that maybe we should meet in Singapore before flying out. He turned down my suggestion. So, on the early morning of 18 May, I was ready to go to India with somebody whom I did not know how he looked like, nor was I certain that he would turn up. Looking back, I must had been crazy to go on a trip like this. Normally, I am a very conservative person, but the craze of seeing Baba prompted me to take risks well beyond the norm. Arriving at the Singapore airport, waiting in the queue to be checked-in, two ladies (Sisters Chow and Tow) approached me informing me that they were Sai devotees and were also going for the Buddha Purnima festival. Sister Chow was a long-time devotee, having visited Baba and served at the Whitefield hospital many, many times. Later, these two sisters turned out to be my saviors in India. At the time, I shared with them that I did not have accommodation in Whitefield. They said that they were staying at Gokulum, Whitefield and there was a possibility of getting me an apartment there. I thought my accommodation problem was solved even before I left Singapore.

After checking-in, I proceeded to the waiting room where I finally met Brother Ananda and his wife, Sister Lalitha. Since we did our check-in separately, we were sitting in different parts of the plane. During the flight, I only had one conversation with Brother Ananda. Upon landing at the Bangalore airport, since Brother Ananda and his wife were going to a hotel in Whitefield and I was going to Bangalore, we took separate taxis, and there was no arrangement for future meeting. So essentially, I was a lone ranger on this trip. How amazing! I went to see Baba for the first time and I went alone.

After arriving at the Bangalore hotel, I took lunch and a rest. In the afternoon, the driver

brought me to the Whitefield ashram, Brindavan.
When I first saw the place, I could not believe it
because it was so old and run-down. I mean this is
the famous Baba ashram, and people traveled
thousands of miles to come here, right? Indeed, with
the non-attractive physical appearance of the
ashram, it actually pronounced even more strongly
how amazing Baba's spiritual attraction is!
Although the place is old, it is filled with Baba's
loving energy. I subsequently found out that this
energy could stay with me even after I returned to
Singapore. Anyway, I went in, joined a queue and
then sat on a bench. As it turned out years later,
this was a rare occasion that I managed to sit on a
bench, because the bench was usually reserved for
devotees who had difficulties sitting on the floor. I
waited and not too long after, Baba came out on a
wheel chair and sat on the veranda. He did not say
anything, stayed for about 30 minutes, and then
went back to his residence. This was my first
darshan (seeing God). So, I arrived in India on
18 May 2005 and saw Baba on the same day. When
Baba called, things could happen very quickly. I
wondered what was all the talk about long queue
and long wait. None of these happened to me during
my first darshan. When I saw Baba for the first
time, I thought he looked really ordinary, just like
any old man. Later, I understood that it is not the
physical appearance but the spiritual heart that is

important which is the extraordinary attraction of Baba.

After the darshan, I went to Gokulum to look for Sisters Chow and Tow. On the way, I met Brother Ananda who then helped me to look for accommodation in Whitefield. Upon reaching Gokulum, they said that they did not have room available and directed us to a house behind the hotel where Brother Ananda was staying. We saw the lady of the house, and she said that there would be a room available the next morning. As it turned out, the owner of this house was Baba's chauffeur. So, I went back to the Bangalore hotel that evening, and was ready to move to Whitefield the next day!

The next day came, after morning darshan and according to plan, I moved to a room in Baba's chauffeur's house. Wow, this must be the barest room I had ever stayed in up to that point in my life. Inside the room, there was one bed which had one bed-sheet, one blanket and one pillow. There was one built-in wardrobe, and one ceiling fan. No chair, no table and no other furniture. There was a connecting room with shower and toilet, but no soap, towel or even toilet paper. There was of course no TV, no computer, no telephone, no kettle, and no laundry service. Talking about minimal materialism, this was it. I mean I came from a rich family and was used to average or well above average physical comfort, like 5-star hotels.

Incredibly, Baba put me here, and this experience completely transformed me.

On this trip, I noticed that although India was materially poor, they were spiritually very rich. This is in stark contrast to Singapore which is materially rich but spiritually very poor. Out of these two types of societies, I prefer the former because you can gain bliss. After you gain bliss, you can gain peace, and then you can practice love. For the latter type, at best you can gain is some short-term, temporal happiness which is a very poor substitute for bliss. Also, with materialism, your desire of wanting more and more will drive you to misery because there is no way to satisfy your insatiable desires. Materialism will also cause fear, because you will be fearful of losing your material riches. Yet there is no way to guard against such loss. So, you can never gain peace, and without peace, you cannot practice love. Since the whole world, except for a few isolated communities, is moving towards materialism, this is why there is so little love in this world. Indeed Baba explained that this is the very reason why he had come. In his 23 November 1968 discourse entitled *"The Milestone Speech"* which appeared in Samuel Sandweiss' book entitled *"Sai Baba – Holy Man and the Psychiatrist"*, he said:

"For the protection of the virtuous, for the destruction of evil-doers and for establishing righteousness on a firm footing. I incarnate from age to age. Whenever disharmony (asanthi) overwhelms the world, the Lord will incarnate in human form to establish the modes of earning peace (prasanthi) and to reeducate the human community in the paths of peace."

After I moved to the room in Baba's chauffeur's house, I was quite concerned because first, I was used to taking supper (late night meal). Usually if I did not take supper, I could not sleep. Then, I noticed that the room was actually opposite to the hotel's kitchen where the light and sound would come into the room until well past midnight. I usually need a dark and quiet environment to sleep. I really wondered if I could sleep well in this room. As it happened, I slept very well throughout the trip except for the first night. The light and sound did not bother me. I also did not feel hungry at night nor crave for supper. When we enter Baba's fold, I find that he would ensure that we are alright. This is Baba's attraction.

However, on the first night, I completely could not sleep because of many, many mosquito bites. Also, I was extremely worried that I might get sick and there was nobody to look after me. I mean I

23

was only at the beginning of the trip and there were many more days to go. Worried and unable to sleep, I cried out to Baba asking, "I've come all this way to see you. Why is this happening to me?" He sent me a reply in the morning. The next day after the morning darshan, I met Sisters Chow and Tow. Then, Sister Chow said to me, "Baba told me that you didn't sleep well last night." I was completely stunned, looking at her with my mouth open. I was thinking, "How did you know?" She explained that during the morning darshan, Baba sent her a message spiritually that I did not sleep well last night. That was why she said to me, "Baba told me that you didn't sleep well last night." Then, I understood why I could not sleep that night. It was Baba's way of telling me that he knew I was there. See how Baba can speak to us through another person. Subsequently, Sisters Chow and Tow advised me to burn candle and incense to prevent further disturbance by the mosquitoes.

After solving the mosquito problem, I had to attend to my other personal needs. By this time, Brother Ananda and his wife were too busy with the preparation of the festival, so I was left completely on my own. While it was not difficult to look for basics like bottled water, soap and toilet paper, I did not know where to get towels. As it happened so often, Baba sent the right person at the right time. An auto rickshaw driver showed me where to get towels, helped me to negotiate price, and we became friends. After a few days of attending darshans, I felt bored. Since I was acquainted with the rickshaw driver, one afternoon I decided to go with him to look around Whitefield. He showed me the bank for Sai donation, a Sai hospital, a river and a school. It was a most delightful tour, and we took many photographs. On my subsequent trips to see Baba, I found out that some of these rickshaw drivers could be very dishonest and nasty. As it happened, I was blessed with a decent rickshaw driver, and to him, I am forever grateful.

By this time, I had plenty of time on my hand. In Whitefield, there was really very little to do, except for darshan which usually lasted between one to two hours. I did not dare to venture out too far because I was alone in a foreign land. I did not really know anyone either. But with Baba's planning, see how he prepared me even before this trip. Eight months earlier in September 2004, as part of my university's student recruitment drive, I had the opportunity to visit different parts of India. This was unusual because in the past, I was not selected. In addition, the recruitment drive included many other countries. So out of all these countries, I managed to go to India. Whatever I learnt about India from the university trip became very useful as I was a lone ranger on this trip. I find that Baba really prepares us for our challenges, and only when we are ready, then we face them - this is another attraction of Baba.

Being alone and not knowing where to go or what to do, I was struggling and desperate. Initially, I tried to sleep it off, but really there were too many hours. I finally entertained the idea that I should go home early – even missing the Buddha Purnima festival which was a major objective of the trip. I wanted to discuss it with somebody, but there was nobody except Sisters Chow and Tow. So one evening, I stumbled into their room. I told them that I was fed up, and wanted to go home. Sister Chow then counseled and encouraged me to stay as the Buddha Purnima festival was only a few days away. She also informed me that I could register with the Singapore group so that I could sit near the front, closer to Baba during the festival. She further explained that this was only possible for devotees from Buddhist countries because it was a Buddha festival. As it was true that the festival was only a few days away and it would be a hassle to change my flight, I accepted her advice and stayed. This decision turned out to be a wonderful blessing because Baba really showered his grace on me later. To Sister Chow, I am forever grateful.

Having decided to stay, I started looking for the Singapore group leader (Brother Vashdev). I went to his room; he was not there. The person inside told me to go back later. I went to his room again, he was not there. The person inside again told me to go back later, and this happened a few times. After a while, I got frustrated. Later, I found out that

Brother Vashdev was a "big-shot" in the Sai organization, and he had "important" duties. Despite all the frustration, I met another devotee (Brother Esvaran) while looking for Brother Vashdev, who turned out to be another of my saviors on this trip. Eventually, I met Brother Vashdev not at his room but at the ashram, and I was registered.

Among all the darshans, there was one which was particularly memorable. During this darshan, when Baba was at the veranda, I had this overwhelming feeling of unconditional love, which I had never felt before. I had tears of joy in my eyes, and I felt the love of Baba. While I was immersed in this unconditional love, I was prepared to give up everything and nothing seemed important anymore. This is another big attraction of Baba – unconditional love.

Towards the end of my trip, one day I had the following spiritual communication with Baba. I said, "Baba, I have come to see you and I'm not asking for any blessing. If you like to give it to me, it's fine. If you don't like to give it to me, it's fine too. Anyway, you know what is best for me". Then I added, "I don't want any physical object". I did not ask for any blessing because I too would not like people coming to see me, and every time they ask for something. I specifically said that I did not want a physical object because I figured that if I got a physical object from Baba (not that it was likely), I

27

would be so afraid of losing it; it would become a burden for the rest of my life. Anyway, as it happened, Baba showered plenty of blessings on me. Moreover, without any direct contact, he managed to give me something and it was indeed not a physical object. It happened on the last day of my trip. So, he really heard my communication and responded accordingly!

Finally, it was my last day of this visit, and it was 23 May 2005 which was the day of the Buddha Purnima festival. Prior to the festival, we were discussing whether he would give a discourse. While he would usually give a discourse during a festival, but on this occasion, he was recovering from a recent fall, so there was uncertainty. To our delight, he did give a discourse entitled *"Develop the Spirit of Oneness"*. So in addition to darshan (seeing God), I also had shravanam (listening to God), and all these happened during my first visit. This was significant because even with all my subsequent visits, this was the only occasion that I had the opportunity to listen to Baba. He concluded his discourse with the bhajan *"Prema Mudita Manase Kaho..."*. After the main events, we all moved to a small auditorium where there was a cultural show. Inside the auditorium, Baba was sitting on the front row with the audience, and I was sitting behind, less than ten feet away from him.

After the festival, I was scheduled to fly back to Singapore on a midnight flight. I had made arrangements for a taxi to bring me to the airport. When the time came, I got into a car which I thought was just an ordinary taxi. After we drove off, I started chatting with the driver. In the middle of our conversation, he asked "Do you know you're in my boss' car?" I quizzed, "Who is your boss?" I then figured out that his boss was Baba's chauffeur. So, the car I was in was the car Baba's chauffeur would use to drive Baba around. So, it was like Baba's car. Isn't it amazing that I actually ended up sitting in Baba's car going to the airport? Remember earlier I communicated to Baba that I did not want any physical object. So, he gave me the experience of sitting in his car! On hindsight, the accommodation problem I had on this visit was a prelude to this divine experience.

After arriving at the airport, I found out that my flight was delayed. It would now depart at 3 a.m. instead of midnight, and I was stuck at the airport. Again, Baba sent me the right person at the right time. At the airport, I saw many Singapore Sai devotees but I did not know any of them, except for Brother Esvaran. Because of him, I got to know the others, and we had wonderful spiritual conversations (satsang). Brother Esvaran even briefed me about Puttaparthi, and advised me if I go there, I should go with someone who had been there before. His advice seemed so irrelevant at the time because I thought I waited for so many years before I could come to Whitefield. I probably have to wait for many more years before I could go to Puttaparthi. Little did I know that with Baba's plan, I actually ended up in Puttaparthi the following year. The three hours passed quickly, and it was a real blessing to have had the opportunity to converse with these devotees.

I finally returned home on 24 May 2005.

Chapter 4

Post first visit

After coming back to Singapore, I found that my visit to Baba did not end there, even though my body had left India. Periodically, the vision of the Whitefield ashram would appear, and my spirit (atma) would visit the ashram, and this happened again and again. I also carried plenty of Baba's energy back with me such that I was highly charged. This level of energy stayed with me for at least six months after my return to Singapore. Since I was at such a high level of energy, I was eager to share my experiences with Brother Ho since he was the instigator, and also with the Friday group. So, I called Brother Ho and volunteered to give a spiritual talk. During the telephone conversation, I found out that at a recent annual general meeting, he had stepped down after being the Chairman for ten years or more. He said that if I wished to give the talk to the Friday group, I had to contact the new Chairman, Brother Tay. I called Brother Tay and he readily accepted my offer of giving a spiritual talk, and it was scheduled for 24 June 2005. The talk was highly charged and throughout the talk, I felt Baba's presence. He was standing next to me giving me all the inspirations. This is another attraction of Baba – he supports us in our endeavors. During the talk, the "real" speaker was of course Baba, and I was merely an instrument. That explained why the talk was so inspiring and full of energy. The group was mesmerized. Afterwards, they all came to touch me thinking that Baba had given me so many blessings, which he did! Since the talk went so well, at the end of it, I made a wish to Baba that I could repeat the talk on another occasion. I did not really expect the wish to come true, but it did.

A few weeks later, Brother Tay on his own initiative asked me if I could give a talk as part of Baba's 80th Birthday Celebrations, and this time the talk was to the general public. I was astounded and happy that Baba responded to my wish. See how Baba picked such an auspicious occasion. With great pleasure and devotion, I repeated the talk on 21 November 2005.

Chapter 5

Second visit

After the first visit, I was keen to go and see Baba again, especially at Puttaparthi. This was unusual for me because as I mentioned before, for "religious" gatherings, usually I would attend once and would not go again. But for Baba, the attractions were too strong! Anyway, even though I was keen, I did not really know when I would get another chance. I was basically back to square one where I needed to find someone to bring me. However, this time the feeling was different, because by now I figured that if it were Baba's will that I should go, he would send me the right person at the right time, and indeed he did.

On 11 February 2006, as part of the Chinese New Year celebration, Brother Tay organized a big reunion dinner for Sai devotees, and he also made the sitting arrangement. Of all the devotees there, I ended up sitting next to Brother Gurunathan whom I did not know before. On hindsight, I could see that sitting next to Brother Gurunathan was no coincidence, but Baba's arrangement. We started chatting and I gathered that he was another long-time devotee. He had been to Puttaparthi many times, and owned a room inside the ashram. He mostly traveled alone and would usually go in July. He casually remarked that I could go with him next time. I did not take that remark seriously then, and months passed.

In May 2006, I started thinking that maybe I could contact Brother Gurunathan to see if he was going in July. But how could I contact him, I did not know his address or telephone number, except I knew that he usually attended the Thursday bhajans. So I went to the Center on Thursdays and for the first couple of weeks, I could not find him. Subsequently, I found him, and indeed he was going to Puttaparthi for the Guru Poornima festival in July, but with seven other devotees. He said that I could join them and we would be traveling in two cars. I welcomed the opportunity, but because of my health problem, I was concerned about traveling with so many strangers and in two cars. As it turned out, my concern was unfounded because four of them subsequently made some other arrangement, and traveled on their own. As for us (i.e. Brother Gurunathan and his wife, Sister Vijaya, Brother Raman and his wife, Sister Sarala, and myself), we would travel in a group of five and in one car. See Baba's attraction in making perfect arrangements.

My second visit was diametrically different from my first. Brother Gurunathan made all the travel and accommodation arrangements for all of us. On the departure date 5 July 2006, we met at the check-in counter, and Brother Gurunathan sat next to me on the plane. He told me his wonderful experiences with Baba (satsang), and this time, I was not alone.

After landing in Bangalore and the long 3-hour drive, we finally reached the Puttaparthi ashram. On the way, we saw Sai Gita (Baba's pet elephant). Little did we know that she was in her final year of present incarnation. Prior to our present visit, Brother Gurunathan had already arranged for two rooms: one for the sisters and one for the brothers. This was my first time staying in an ashram. While the ashram was similarly old and run-down like the one in Whitefield, I was not shocked this time. This ashram was far bigger, like a university campus, and had many more facilities as compared to that in Whitefield. It also had a peaceful and holy atmosphere. Appropriately the name of the ashram was Prasanthi Nilayam (abode of the highest peace). On the other hand, the room was even barer than the one in Whitefield. This room had absolutely nothing except a connecting room with shower and toilet. So we laid three mattresses on the floor and that was our "palace". So, I basically slept on the floor with two strangers throughout this visit. How extraordinary? I happily accepted a situation which under normal circumstance I would have objected strongly! See the power of Baba's attraction. With love and spirituality, material comfort becomes so unimportant. Another extraordinary thing about the room was its rate: less than US$1 per person per night, and it was sufficient to cover the running cost of the room. Isn't this incredible? Could this happen anywhere else?

By the time we got settled down, the afternoon darshan was over, so we did not see Baba on the first day. That evening, Brother Raman and his wife went out with another group, so only three of us were left contemplating whether we should go out for dinner. Brother Gurunathan was actually very tired because he watched the World Cup soccer match the night before and had very little sleep. So he really wanted to go straight to bed without dinner. But then he realized that since I did not have dinner, I must be hungry. So even with his tiredness, Brother Gurunathan brought me to have a good dinner. In fact, Brother Gurunathan took care of everything throughout the trip, which included all the meals, laundry, and sightseeing. In addition, he got us tickets so that we could sit near the front during darshan without queuing. I am forever grateful to Brother Gurunathan.

Since Brother Gurunathan arranged for all the meals, for lunch, we usually ate at the Western Canteen inside the ashram. For the evening meals,

however, we would usually go out and Brother
Gurunathan loved the chapattis at an Indian
restaurant operated by Baba's ex-gardener. I mean
I was used to Chinese diet, so it was unimaginable to
have Indian food every night. Similar to my first
visit, there were things that would normally bother
me, but during my visits to Baba, they did not
bother me at all.

After the first day, we had darshan everyday.
During each darshan and on non-festival days, it
can easily attract tens of thousands of devotees, and
on festival days, it can attract millions. Isn't this
incredible? What kind of worldly activity can
attract these numbers of people day in, day out and
at a frequency of once in the morning and once in
the afternoon? During non-festival days, in a way,
it is even more incredible because there is usually no
show, no discourse, and Baba may appear for less
than 20 minutes. Yet people came and some waited
for hours for his appearance. On one occasion, I
witnessed Baba come to the veranda and then go
straight into the interview room. So his appearance
was less than two minutes. Yet after seeing Baba for
such a brief moment, the devotees looked so blissful,
and then happily dispersed to carry on with their
own businesses. This truly epitomizes the greatness
in Baba's attraction!

On 7 July 2006, it was the Ashadi Ekadashi
festival during which two musical dramas were
presented. One in the morning entitled "*The Divine*

Commandment *'I am I — Aham Asmi Aham'* ", and one in the afternoon entitled *"The Ten Commandments"*. Between the two dramas, Brothers Gurunathan, Raman and I had time to visit the Chaitanya Museum.

Two days later, on 9 July 2006, Brother Gurunathan took me on a sightseeing trip in which we visited the Siva Mandir, Samadhi and the Kalpa Vruksha Tree.

Finally, it was the Guru Poornima festival on 11 July 2006, which was a major objective of this trip. I really felt blessed that I was able to witness two festivals within one single trip. The celebrations for the festival actually commenced the evening before with a music programme by the Bailey sisters. The next day, on the morning of 11 July, Baba blessed around 50 physically challenged people with tricycles to enable them to live a more independent life. See how Baba practices compassion. In the afternoon, the Sai Symphony Orchestra performed. It had 67 members coming from 22 countries. Can you believe that, members from 22 different countries? Where else can this happen?

On the same day between the morning and afternoon darshans, because Brothers Gurunathan and Raman had their own activities, I was left on my own, and I had time. How should I spend my time? It suddenly dawned on me that I could visit the library inside the ashram. During the library visit, I discovered that apart from the book entitled "*Man of Miracles*", Howard Murphet had written many other books. See how Baba guides us to the right reading material. Today, I have a full collection of his books, and he was a real bringer of the "light". To Howard Murphet, I am forever grateful.

After the festival and during our last couple of days on this trip, Brother Gurunathan noticed that a garland that he had placed on a Baba photograph in his room, grew longer and longer (front cover of this book). It is said that this is Baba's way to show his "welcome". So, he sent us his blessings before we left India.

Finally, we returned to Singapore on 13 July 2006. Similar to my first visit, I carried Baba's energy back with me. Periodically, the vision of a path inside the ashram would appear, and my spirit (atma) would walk the path again and again. The energy stayed with me for several months after my return.

How Sai Baba attracts without direct contact

Chapter 6

First visit by Baba in dream

On 7 December 2005, I was involved in a car accident in which both cars were badly damaged. While I contended that the other car hit mine, the other driver thought that I was in the wrong. After the accident, I proceeded to make my insurance claim against the other driver. Nothing was heard and my no-claim bonus was intact when I renewed my insurance in May 2006. So, I thought everything was settled and the other driver did not claim against me. Then I got a shock on 23 November 2006 (Baba's birthday) when a man from a law firm came to my apartment and delivered a writ of summons. I was very concerned because I was afraid that I had to go to court.

The next day, during the very early hours of 24th, I was sleeping next to my wife. As I rolled over and my hair touched hers, I felt her body changed and it was a body that wore an orange robe and with fuzzy hair. At the time, I thought it was very strange that my wife would dress like that because it was totally unlike her. Only after I had woken up that I realized Baba had come and he superimposed himself on to my wife's body. He was sleeping next to me, and my hair touched his. He had come to comfort me only hours after I received the writ of summons.

Despite Baba's visit, for days after I received the writ of summons, I was losing sleep. About one week after the first delivery and on 4 December 2006, the man came again and delivered a second writ of summons, which was unusual. During the second delivery, the man said to me "Don't lose sleep over this." When I heard these words, I understood why there was this second delivery. Baba wanted to speak to me through this man, and he was helping me to get over the predicament. This is another of Baba's attraction – when we are in trouble, he comes and helps.

And since the second delivery, I have not heard about the summons anymore.

Chapter 7

Third visit

Although I started attending bhajans in 2003, my wife Christina did not join me apart from a few isolated occasions. So I was basically attending bhajans on my own and it lasted for more than two years. During that period, from time to time during bhajans, I wished to Baba that my wife would be there with me. Completely without any persuasion on my part, suddenly one day in early 2007, Christina said that she would join me in attending bhajans on a regular basis. There was no sign prior to her announcement; so it came as a total surprise to me. I was absolutely delighted that Baba has finally called her. See when Baba calls, they will come, and it can happen suddenly. Anyway, Christina's explanation was that since we were both growing old, it would be better for us to join the same group rather than different group. Christina was joining a Buddhist group at that time, and she left them for Baba.

After attending bhajans regularly, Christina was then keen to go to India to see Baba. Since I have been to Whitefield and Puttaparthi already, and now I have Christina as my companion, I did not need to find someone to bring me there anymore. On the other hand, if we both go, we had to choose a period when we could be sure that our family would be safe during our absence. The best period is June because it is the traditional month for the school holidays in Singapore. After my two trips to see Baba, I was still eager to go. In fact, I felt more excited this time because Christina was joining me. Hence, we planned to go in June 2007 and that would be just two of us. A few weeks prior to the trip, one day after bhajans, we casually mentioned to a few devotees that we were going to see Baba on our own. One of the devotees, Sister Pek Moon expressed her interest in joining us. At work, Christina also casually mentioned to her colleagues that she was going to see Baba. One of her colleagues, Sister Lin Dai also expressed her interest in joining us. So completely unsolicited, our group grew from two to four. Also instead of other people bringing me to see Baba, I was now bringing others to see Baba. See how Baba gives us opportunities to serve when we are ready. I felt truly blessed and was determined to look after them the best I could. While Sister Pek Moon had seen Baba once before, my wife Christina and Sister Lin Dai would be seeing Baba for the first time.

As I had the responsibility of bringing three ladies to see Baba, and I was not exactly a seasoned traveler to India, I thought I better contact my ex-colleague, Dr. Appan, whom I knew has a brother living in Bangalore. So I called up Dr. Appan and got his brother's name and telephone number, which was a precautionary measure in case we needed help in India. During our telephone conversation, I found out that by coincidence he was also going to India around the same period as we were going. I did not take too much notice of the coincidence at the time but subsequently, it proved to be a divine arrangement which saved our day.

Prior to departure on 6 June 2007, I was actually thinking what would be the best sitting arrangement for the four of us on the plane. I then had the vision that the three ladies would sit in one row and I would get an aisle seat on the row behind them. When we were checking-in at the airport, the airline staff told me that the best sitting arrangement she could do was either

(1) three of us seat in one row, but the fourth would sit some distance away, or

(2) two of us sit together in one row, the third and fourth would sit one row behind but separated by the aisle.

Out of these two options, I chose the first because I thought it would be better for the ladies to sit together so that they would enjoy the flight better. I would then sit on my own on another part of the plane. So the seating arrangement was settled, and I was not concerned. But then I had a strange feeling:

(1) How come the vision I had did not materialize?

(2) When we got to the airport, it was quite early so there should be many seats available. How come we did not get my preferred seating?

Anyway after we had checked-in, we proceeded to the waiting room. While we were there, we saw one Sai devotee rushing in. He was Brother Chandran from the Friday group whom I knew by face but not by name. We happily chatted and saying how good it was that we were all going to Puttaparthi on the same flight. While we were walking to board the plane, I casually asked him what was his seat number, and he said "20D". I could not believe it because the seat numbers for the three ladies were 19D, 19E and 19F. His seat was an aisle seat, one row behind the ladies'. He willingly exchanged the seat with mine which was "12D". So finally, my vision and preferred seating materialized. Then, I understood why I did not get my preferred seating in the first place. It was Baba's way of telling me that he knew I was there, and also his way of giving me blessings. So unlike the second visit when Baba

46

gave me blessings towards the end of the trip, on this third visit he gave me blessings at the beginning of the trip.

After landing at Bangalore, Brother Chandran took his pre-arranged taxi, and we took ours to Puttaparthi. At about half-way point, we stopped at a café for lunch. Some time later and without prior arrangement, Brother Chandran rushed in and he was so happy to see us. Apparently, he forgot to bring any Indian rupees with him, and he was hoping to find us there so that we could pay for his lunch. We were delighted to be saviors for our fellow devotee for a change.

After arriving at Puttaparthi and checking into a hotel, we still had time to attend the afternoon darshan. So my wife Christina and Sister Lin Dai saw Baba for the first time on 6 June 2007. Throughout the trip, I took care of everything, and we visited many places, including all the places that I visited during my second visit. In addition, we visited the Sri Sathya Sai Hill View Stadium, the Eternal Heritage Museum, the General Hospital, the Chitravathi River and the newly built Indoor Games Complex for Students, and the Abode of Sai Gita (Baba's pet elephant who left his physical incarnation on 22 May 2007 shortly before our visit). During the sightseeing, we noticed that along the main road leading to the ashram, posters were displayed and they contained words of wisdom. The following saying caught my attention:

> *"You will be guided,*
> *However far you be geographically,*
> *I am as near to you as you are near to*
> *me."*

So we attended darshans everyday and during one darshan, Sister Pek Moon and my wife Christina actually witnessed Baba materialize a necklace for a little girl. To be able to witness a live materialization, they felt that they were blessed by Baba. On another day, we went to the Western Canteen for lunch. We arrived early. I was waiting outside the men's entrance, and Sisters Pek Moon, Lin Dai and my wife Christina were waiting outside the ladies' entrance. Just before the canteen was due to open, a seva dal (devotee doing volunteer work) came out from the ladies' entrance and asked for volunteers to help to serve food. The number of volunteers she wanted - exactly three! Without hesitation, my wife and the two sisters grabbed the opportunity. Again, they felt that they were blessed by Baba because it is usually difficult to get opportunity to do seva inside the ashram. Yet for Sister Lin Dai and my wife Christina, it was their first visit and they have done seva inside the ashram. See how Baba attracts without direct contact.

After settling down, I thought of calling up Dr. Appan who also should be in India then. This was unusual for me because I am not the type who likes to make social calls. Anyway, I did call and he was indeed in India but due to fly back to Singapore the next day. So I got him just in time and this call proved to be significant later. During the telephone conversation, he told me that one of our ex-colleagues, Dr. Pandey, was working in a university in Bangalore. Dr. Pandey moved from Singapore back to India some 20 years ago, and throughout this period, neither Dr. Appan nor myself had communicated with him. So it was most unusual that Dr. Appan would make the effort to look up Dr. Pandey's telephone number through a third party, and then call him later. In any case, he passed me Dr. Pandey's telephone numbers, and then he left India. Like I said, I am not the type who likes to make social calls. So for some inexplicable reason, I called Dr. Pandey and we made an arrangement to meet at the Bangalore airport prior to our departure back to Singapore.

Everything went smoothly, until our second last day in Puttaparthi. On that day, after the afternoon darshan, we got separated and Christina was going back to the hotel on her own. To go from the ashram to the hotel, there was a short cut through a small narrow lane. While she was walking through this lane, three men of which two were rickshaw drivers approached her and asked for money. These rickshaw drivers knew us because we had previously hired them for sightseeing. Christina ignored them and quickly went back to the hotel. Some time later, Sisters Pek Moon and Lin Dai were also going back to the hotel. The three men also approached them for money at the small lane. After the three of them got back to the hotel, they grouped together and came out to look for me. I met them at the small lane and those men were again there, and they also asked me for money. We did not give them any and hurried back to the hotel.

When we were having supper that evening, we discussed what we should do. Since those men were always hanging around at the hotel entrance, if we go out, we feared that they would do something to us. I figured that the safest thing to do would be to stay inside the hotel until we were due to go to Bangalore airport the next day. But then we would be stuck inside the hotel for the whole day. Alternatively, we could leave Puttaparthi the next morning, and then spend the whole day in Bangalore until our midnight flight to Singapore. But then what would we do in Bangalore and where could we go? Also, if we wanted to take a rest in Bangalore, it would be expensive to stay in a hotel there. As we were struggling to find a solution, Baba sent us his savior. Since Dr. Appan passed me Dr. Pandey's telephone numbers, both office and home, I could actually call him that evening. Indeed, I did and he was free to meet us the next day at his university. Without Dr. Pandey, we would have to make a difficult decision, and potentially the trip could end with much unpleasantness. As it was, we left Puttaparthi the next morning with great relief and arrived at Bangalore at mid-day. Dr. Pandey provided us lunch and on his own initiative, he also booked a guest room for us. So we got some rest, had a tour of the university and then had some more sightseeing on our way to the airport. The arrangement was perfect. I am forever grateful to Dr. Pandey. See all the inexplicable phone calls, they all happened for a reason. This is another of Baba's attraction - he prompts us to take appropriate actions.

While we were at the Bangalore airport waiting to be checked in, we met a lady who was also a Singapore Sai devotee. She told us that she was traveling alone, she was not well and needed help. In fact, she was hesitant to make the return trip on her own but spiritually, Baba assured her that he would send her saviors, and everything would be alright. We were her saviors and accompanied her all the way back to Singapore. This is another attraction of Baba – he allows us to be saviors.

Finally, we returned to Singapore safely on 12 June 2007. On the next day 13 June 2007, I gave a talk to the Wednesday group of which Brother Ho was the chairman.

Similar to my first two visits, I carried Baba's energy back with me. Periodically, the vision of a bookshop just outside the ashram would appear, and my spirit (atma) would hang around that area again and again. The energy stayed with me for several months after my return.

Chapter 8

Fourth visit and second visit by Baba in dream

Despite the anxious moments during our trip in 2007, the attractions of Baba were so strong that in early 2008, we (Sisters Pek Moon and Lin Dai, my wife Christina and I) were already planning for another trip in May that year. At the planning stage, Baba proved his saying (*Sanathana Sarathi*, August 1984):

"Love my uncertainty."

In March 2008, unexpectedly, my doctor informed me that my prostate had become so large that most probably, I needed an operation. He also advised me that it was better to have the operation at my earliest convenience, which would be in April. As it was not advisable to travel shortly after the operation, I thought the trip was off. After seeing Baba for three consecutive years, I thought I had to reluctantly take a break in 2008. Upon the next consultation, the doctor confirmed that the operation was the best course of action. Again unexpectedly, he suggested that I could take a medicine for three months, which would ease the operation. Hence, the operation was postponed to July. So suddenly, my trip to see Baba was on again - Baba's leela on uncertainty.

Upon hearing the news of the operation, I was quite concerned about the cost as it would amount to more than ten thousand Singapore dollars (seven thousand U.S. dollars). My insurance policy would only cover a small fraction of the cost. Out of the blue, my employer came up with a new medical scheme in which most of the hospitalization cost would be covered, and the new scheme would be effective from July 2008 (the month of my operation). This is another attraction of Baba - he really looks after our needs. In fact, the entire hospitalization cost was subsequently covered under the new medical scheme.

So the trip was fixed for 26-30 May 2008, and two more friends joined us (Sisters Ah Nya and Yi Ping). Both of them had not seen Baba before. I felt so blessed that I was able to bring these people to see Baba. We initially planned to go to Whitefield. Upon hearing Baba went from Puttaparthi to Whitefield on 26 April, and likely to stay there for more than one month, we thought our trip to Whitefield was assured. For less than one week, on 2 May, we suddenly heard that Baba had left

Whitefield and had gone back to Puttaparthi. Well, we thought Baba would surely stay there now and would not visit Whitefield again in 2008. Our plan was therefore changed, and we were going to Puttaparthi. To our total surprise, Baba went from Puttaparthi to Whitefield again on 21 May – another Baba's leela on uncertainty.

So finally, we went to Whitefield, and this was the first time for all the ladies. As the new Bangalore airport had only opened a few days before our departure, we enjoyed to be among the first devotees to land there. On our first day in Whitefield, we managed to attend the afternoon darshan. So Sisters Ah Nya and Yi Ping saw Baba for the first time on 26 May 2008.

Throughout the trip, six of us stayed in one apartment and it was a beautiful apartment – well furnished and well equipped. It was near hotels where we could get our meals and about a 10-minute walk to the ashram. This was a far cry from the living conditions during my first two visits. In spirituality, however, we live in equanimity irrespective of the physical conditions. This is another attraction of Baba – he guides us to live in equanimity.

Similar to my third visit, I took care of everything and looked after them the best I could. Not forgetting the kindness Dr. Pandey showed us during our last visit, I made the effort to go to Bangalore and thanked him profusely.

So we were happily staying at Whitefield and attending darshans everyday. On the way to the ashram and back to the apartment, we actually walked through the ground of Sri Sathya Sai Institute of Higher Learning (which was renamed as the Sri Sathya Sai University on 2 February 2007). Stone plagues were placed along the path and they contained words of wisdom. The following saying caught my attention:

> *"When you lose your wealth, you lose nothing.*
> *When you lose your health, you lose something.*
> *When you lose your character, you lose everything."*

After a few days in Whitefield, we were nearing the end of our trip, and the following incident happened. During the early morning on 29 May 2008 just before waking time, I dreamt of a tall, slim, elderly person who appeared like a wise guru. He was dressed in shirt and trousers, completely unlike Baba. We sat at a square table, he was on my right discussing the ideas in my article entitled *"How to become a master of life"*. He was supportive of the ideas. The vision from the dream was clear and vivid, and stayed with me for many months thereafter. During the dream, I had no idea that the elderly person was Baba. Only after I woke up and later during that day, in the vision, the elderly person transformed himself to Baba. Then, I realized that the person in my dream was Baba, and he had come to give blessings to the article. This was Baba's response to the article which I sent him on 2 May 2008, just before this trip. See how exacting was the response:

(1) He came into my dream when I was in Whitefield, and not in Singapore.
(2) The content of the dream was on the article, and not on something else.

This is another attraction of Baba - he gives blessings in dreams.

Finally, we returned to Singapore on 30 May 2008. Upon our return, I carried Baba's energy from the dream and I was highly charged. The energy stayed for more than one year.

Since the completion of my article entitled *"How to become a master of life"* which was some time ago, I tried many ways to get it published as a book but to no avail. All possible avenues appeared to have been exhausted and I really thought that it would never get published. Little did I know then, it was meant to be part of this book that you are reading now – see the divine plan, Baba blessed the article and it is now in Appendix B of this book. This is another attraction of Baba – if we do our best, he will do the rest.

How Sai Baba attracts without direct contact

Chapter 9

Visits by Baba during operations

Throughout my life, except at birth, I have never been hospitalized and also never had operation. During the years 2007-2008, however, I had three operations within eight months. These were deeply stressful experiences for me, so I prayed to Baba. This is another attraction of Baba – when we pray, he will come (in spirit).

For many years and for many times, I have played basketball with my three sons on Saturday evenings, which were usually full of fun and free of injury. On 1 December 2007, we played our normal basketball game. Towards the end of the game when Lester and I were competing for the ball, he hit my left hand and I felt a sharp pain in one of my fingers. I retired from the game and the pain persisted for a while and then subsided. After returning home, we all thought that it was probably a minor injury which did not warrant a visit to the accident and emergency department at a hospital that evening. The next morning, my wife accompanied me to see a doctor at a local clinic. The doctor examined my finger and concluded that since I did not feel pain, probably there was no fracture. However, as a precaution, she advised me to take an x-ray the next day. As the next day was a Monday and I had work to do in the morning, I only went for the x-ray in the afternoon. The x-ray showed that I had a diagonal fracture in my left ring finger. The doctor referred me to a specialist and he confirmed that with this type of fracture, I needed an operation. Indeed, I had the operation that Monday evening on 3 December 2007 under general anesthetic. During the operation, I did not pray to Baba because I was unconscious. Recalling the events leading to the operation, all the doctors agreed that with fractured finger, there should be severe pain. Yet for two days, I was going about my business with a fractured finger and I felt no pain. This is another attraction of Baba – he protects us from pain.

After the first operation, the specialist informed me that there were screws and plates inside my finger. For 90% of his patients, they did not need a second operation because for them these screws and plates could stay inside. Although I was hoping that I would be among this 90% group, as it turned out, I was not. During subsequent review sessions, the specialist advised me to have a second operation to remove the screws and plates. So less than three months after my first operation, I was scheduled to have the second operation on 20 February 2008. I was more anxious with the second operation than the first because:

(1) The events leading to the first operation happened so quickly that emotionally, I had no time to respond to it.
(2) I had a major problem with my finger; so I welcomed the operation to solve it.
(3) The operation was done under general anesthetic; so I was unconscious.

On the other hand, with the second operation:

(1) I had plenty of time to think about it (or to avoid it).
(2) I did not have a major problem with my finger and I did not welcome the operation.
(3) The operation would be done under local anesthetic, in fact only on one finger; so I would be conscious during the operation.

Hence, when I laid on the bed in the operating theatre, I was very nervous. What would it be like when they cut open my finger and I was conscious? I could not run away then. I figured that all I could do was pray to Baba. "Come and help me," I said. A few minutes later, a voice came into my head. He said "I'm here". The voice was firm and assuring. When I prayed again, the voice repeated "I'm here", and it happened a few times. As said in the bhajan entitled "*Why Fear When I Am Here*":

> "*Why fear when I am here*
> *So says Baba, Sathya Sai Baba,*
> *Sathya Sai Baba, my Lord*
>
> *Why fear when I am here*
> *All I want is your love my child, all I*
> *want is your faith*
> *All I want is your love in God, no*
> *matter what's your faith*
>
> *Krishna Buddha Jesus Allah, all came*
> *to this land*
> *All of them brought the message of love,*
> *love your fellow men*
>
> *The light you see in the dark of night, is*
> *that of God in man*
> *Find the light that is in your heart, and*
> *reach the promised land*"

I knew then the voice was from Baba, and he was in the operating theatre. He had come to calm me down and comfort me. The operation was successful. This is another attraction of Baba – he gives us emotional support.

After having had two operations in a row, I really did not want another one. Baba, however, gives us what we need, and not what we want – this is another precious attraction of Baba. So in March 2008, when I went for a check-up for my prostate, I was in complete dismay when I heard that I needed another operation. So after all the uncertainties on when to have the operation, it was finally scheduled for 3 July 2008 after my fourth visit. This operation was different from the first two because this was considered a major operation, and I read from a book which said that it could cause death. I was really concerned whether this would be the end of my present incarnation. I was also concerned because this operation would be done not under general anesthetic but half-body anesthetic, which meant only the lower half of my body would be under anesthetic, and I would be conscious during the operation. So, as I laid on a bed in the waiting room outside the operating theatre, I was really nervous and again all I could do was pray to Baba. Then from the corner of my eyes, I saw an orange robe standing about two feet away on the right hand side of my bed. As the nurse pushed me into the operating theatre, I saw the orange robe follow and accompany me into the operating theatre. After I was transferred on to the bed in the operating theatre, I saw the orange robe move to one corner of the operating theatre so that he would not obstruct the medical staff who were working on me. See how considerate was Baba even when he was in spiritual form. So again, he came to calm me down and comfort me when I was in need. I knew then the operation would be successful and it was. Throughout the operation and the post-operation procedures, many people reported pain and discomfort. In my case with the grace of Baba, there was no pain and little discomfort — this is another attraction of Baba.

Chapter 10

Visits by two Ammas and fifth visit

Between 2007-09, the world plunged into the deepest economic recession since the Great Depression of the 1930s. During this period of deep recession, my spiritual activities actually blossom and they came into full bloom in the year 2009.

In March 2009, Sri Mata Amritanandamayi Devi (commonly known as Amma and the hugging saint) visited Singapore. Amma actually had visited Singapore previously but at that time, I did not know her; so I did not meet her. In fact, I only heard of Amma one year earlier in 2008, and it happened not in Singapore but in India during my fourth visit. On that evening, my wife and I were having dinner in a restaurant inside a hotel at Whitefield. As the restaurant was quite full, a French lady wanting a seat shared our table. We started a conversation and found out that this French lady was also a Sai devotee and was very knowledgeable on spiritual matters. She told us many spiritual things which included Amma. She said, "Like Baba, Amma is also an avatar." I am forever grateful to this French lady. To show how spiritually evolved she was, she sold everything in France and moved to Puttaparthi to live on her own, so that she could be closer to Baba on a long term basis. How many people can do that? Anyway, back in Singapore, I enjoyed Amma's darshan on 28 March and had a divine hug on 30 March 2009. On the latter day, I witnessed Amma hugging her devotees continuously without a single break for six hours or more. Is this love in action?

Since 2008, my wife and I have been joining another group for bhajans, namely the Sai Mission group. One day after bhajans, one of their leaders Brother Henry invited me to give a talk. I duly accepted and on 8 April 2009, I shared with them some of my Baba's experiences described in this book. During the talk, I again felt highly charged and inspired, I emphasized that Baba can communicate with us spiritually, and there is no need for direct contact – which is the main message of this book.

Between 16-18 May 2009, we joined a group of Singapore Sai devotees (in particular Brother Kai Cheong and Sister Saw Bee) to visit the Sri Sathya Sai Baba Glugor Center in Penang, Malaysia. This is the famous "miracle house" of Penang. Within this region, no other place has had more miracles than those happened in this house. Miracles include materialization of physical objects, materialization of vibhutti (holy ash), vibhutti appearing inside bottled water, words appearing from vibhutti, and materialization of falling beads. On 16 May, we joined their Center's 29th anniversary celebration, and this year was special because the Center has just been newly renovated. On 17 May, the celebration was over; we went to the Center so that we could do some prayer quietly. In the morning and before we went for our lunch break, we placed some empty containers on the altar. In the evening, when we returned, the containers were filled with vibhutti. We were assured that nobody physically filled the containers with vibhutti; so the containers were filled through materialization. While this materialization of vibhutti was undoubtedly a miracle but it was not convincing because we did not witness it. Then, we came to our last day on this trip. On 18 May, we again went to the Center to do some prayers and were scheduled to leave at 4:30 pm, so that we could catch the evening flight back to Singapore. As we completed our final prayers and were getting ready to leave the Center, Brother Kai Cheong had to pack a Baba photograph because he agreed to bring it back to Singapore for a fellow devotee. As he was doing the packing in front of the altar, suddenly more than 80 beads fell from the ceiling and showered on us. There was also a loud bang and showering sound. Now both the beads and the sound were real miracles because:

(1) We were inside the prayer room which was completely enclosed. So the beads had to come from materialization.

(2) The showering sound of the beads was so loud that it could not have been caused by the beads because they were quite small and the floor was carpeted. So even the sound had to come from materialization.

To add to the miracles, all these happened at around 4:15 pm – a mere 15 minutes before we were due to leave the Center. So just when we thought that nothing would happen, Baba gave us blessings! This is another attraction of Baba.

Towards the end of 2008, I started writing this book, and in May 2009, I thought the book was complete and ready for publication. So, I was looking for a publisher and actually sent a book proposal of this book to a publisher on 21 May 2009. Generally, to get a publisher to accept a book proposal is not easy, and for a spiritual book, it can be even more difficult. This I learned when I was trying to publish the article entitled *"How to become a master of life"*. Nevertheless, through my academic work, I got a book proposal accepted by a publisher, and they appeared to be receptive to all types of proposals. So, I submitted the book proposal to this publisher and I was quite hopeful. On 30 May 2009, I received an email saying that the proposal was rejected. In receiving the news, I was quite despondent because I felt I was stuck. I could not figure out which other publisher would possibly accept this book. I really thought that this was the end, and there was no way to get this book published. Then, just one day after I received the rejection email, I stumbled upon the CreateSpace website. In fact, I found CreateSpace through a Sai book entitled "*Sathya Sai Baba – the Christ of Our Days*" by Vladimir Antonov, which was also published by CreateSpace. It is much easier to publish a book through CreateSpace because it belongs to "self-publishing", which does not require a book proposal to be accepted and so on. On top of that, they use the "print-on-demand" technology, so they do not charge a hefty fee. The only requirement is that the author has to order one proof copy before the book can be listed on the Amazon.com website. This is ideal for me. So I proceeded with submitting the computer file of this book to CreateSpace, and on 16 June 2009, with great elation, I received the first proof copy. I got my Sai Baba book in print – my dream has come true. And all these happened within a mere 3 weeks when I thought the book was dead. See how Baba works, just when I thought I was trapped at a dead end, he pointed me the way – this is another great attraction of Baba.

In July 2009, Sri Narayani Amma visited Singapore, and he is known to cure people with serious illness like cancer without even meeting them. He is also known to know what we are thinking even before we speak. I got to know about Amma's visit through Brother Kai Cheong and enjoyed the first Sri Narayani Amma's darshan on 4 July. See how Baba connects us with the right people – this is another attraction of Baba. If not for the Penang trip in which we became close to Brother Kai Cheong, I would not be aware of Amma's visit. Anyway after the first darshan, I felt the energy was so good that I went for three more darshans during Amma's one week visit. Similar to Baba, Sri Mata Amritanandamayi Devi and now Sri Narayani Amma, I find that when I am close to these divine souls, I can feel the higher, divine energy. Indeed, as we evolve spiritually, we will naturally be attracted to these divine souls.

For the past two years 2007-08, we have been visiting Baba during the months May and June, which are the Singapore school holidays. This year 2009, we planned to do likewise and in fact, it should be easier because only my wife and I were going. As it turned out, there were a lot of happenings in the family that prevented us from leaving Singapore. In fact at one point, it looked like we would not be able to visit Baba at all this year. Just when hope was fading, Baba sent us his savior. In this instance, the savior was none other than my son, Alston. Previously, we could only visit Baba during the school holiday because my wife had to send our sons to school. However, this year is different because Alston passed his driving test on 27 February 2009; so he could take over my wife's duty during her absence. I am forever grateful to Alston.

With great joy and devotion, on 23-27 July 2009, I visited Baba for the fifth time in five consecutive years. Isn't this amazing? I waited for more than 10 years before my first visit, and now I see Baba five years in a row. When we are in touch with Baba, he keeps in touch with us – this is another attraction of Baba.

So we arrived in Puttaparthi on 23 July. Despite two hours delay in flight arrival and doing the necessary administration to get a room inside the ashram, we were still in time for the afternoon darshan. Baba came out in a wheelchair, spent about half an hour talking to devotees, stayed for the bhajans until arathi (the closing prayer song), and then went back to his residence. Like all my previous visits, I felt the loving, divine energy and it was as strong as ever – this is another attraction of Baba.

After the darshan, we went outside the ashram planning to give a telephone call back to Singapore, to get some bottled water, and to have dinner. So we went to one of the best hotels in Puttaparthi, planning to have dinner there. As it happened, there was a power failure and the whole restaurant was dark. We left there and walked further along the

71

street, and saw a place where we could make the telephone call. The place was on a first floor; so we walked upstairs and made the call. Then, there was a restaurant right next to the telephone booth. Since the restaurant was on the first floor, even with the power failure, the restaurant was quite bright. So we settled there to have our dinner. At the end of dinner, I noticed that the restaurant was actually selling some books and maps. I went to take a look and immediately took a liking to the book entitled *"Divine Revelations"* by Sathya Sai Shree Lakshmi. I bought this book and a Puttaparthi map. This was unusual because we were fully aware that there was a bookshop inside the ashram and they sold very good books at very cheap prices. So what prompted me to buy the book? All will be revealed later.

After we went back to the ashram, we prepared our room for the night's rest. The facilities in the room were very basic: two beds, one chair, one table, one ceiling fan, a connecting room with shower and toilet, no soap, no towel and no toilet paper but there are bed sheets and pillows. After so many visits, I was completely used to this minimal materialism, and my wife and I liked it. In fact, I enjoyed coming to see Baba every year because of

(1) Baba's spiritual attraction, and
(2) simple living.

Remember during my first visit, I craved for 5-star hotel comfort, but it means very little to me now. Since then, I am less materialistic, and more spiritual. This is another attraction of Baba – he helps us to become more spiritual.

After we unpacked our things, sorted out other things in the room, took a shower, we were ready to take our rest. Just before the rest, I took out the book "*Divine Revelations*" and read a few pages. To my absolute astonishment, I found the following saying by Baba entitled "*My Vow*", he said:

> "*It is your duty and human right to recognise me and my reality either through this holy book or through your own experience. You will all be saved. Even if you forget me, I will neither forget you nor abandon you. Atheists also are mine. I have incarnated to attract one and all towards myself to give them the assurance that they will be rescued.*
>
> *This is my vow.*"

Notice in the vow, the words "book", "experience", and "attract" are all there. Aren't these the most relevant words of this book? How often will you find a Baba saying which contains all these words in one paragraph? More intriguing is that I did not look for the saying; it fell on to my lap and it happened on the first day of this trip. Isn't the vow aptly applicable to this book? Doesn't this book help to recognize Baba and show his (inner) reality? I then understood why there was the power failure which led us to a different restaurant, and why I bought the book *"Divine Revelations"* under most unusual circumstances. Baba was blessing this book through the vow. With Baba's blessings, the book is complete and ready for publication.

On the next day, my wife and I went for the morning darshan. Baba did not come. In fact, Baba has not been coming out for the morning darshan for many days already. Yet, tens of thousands of devotees were waiting there patiently. This truly epitomizes the attraction of Baba without direct contact! .

Thereafter, we enjoyed two more afternoon darshans, and on 27 July 2009, we returned to Singapore. Upon my return, like all my previous visits, I carried Baba's energy with me. Periodically, the vision of the Sai Kulwant Hall (mandir) would appear, and my spirit (atma) would visit the hall again and again.

On 9 September 2009, this book was finally published, and it is also listed on the Amazon.com website. See how Baba picked such an auspicious date 09.09.09, and 9 is also Baba's number. So Baba is blessing this book again and again and again. Thank you Baba!

Chapter 11

Epilogue

So, what does it mean to be attracted to Baba and to become a devotee? In Baba's discourse on 23 November 1976 entitled *"Signs and Wonders"*, he said:

> *"Why does the Divine attract? Is it to deceive or mislead? No. It is to transform, reconstruct, reform - a process called samskaara. What is the purpose of the reconstruction? To make the person useful and serviceable for society, to efface his ego, and to affirm in him the unity of all beings In God. The person who has undergone samskaara becomes a humble servant of those who need help. This is the stage of paropakaara. Service of this kind done with reverence and selflessness, prepares man to realise the One that pervades the many. The last*

> *stage is saakshaathkaara. The Vedhas (ancient scriptures of Divine Knowledge) proclaim that Immortality (the stage when one is merged in the Birthless, Deathless, Universal Entity), is feasible through renunciation and detachment only, and not through rituals, progeny or wealth. "*

Since becoming a devotee, I can humbly say that I am a transformed human being. The following four incidents illustrate the transformation.

A few years back, my wife and I were going home after a good day out, and we were eager to reach home to take a rest. I was doing the driving and when we were on the last stretch of road leading to our condominium, I saw an object lying on the road. This object was quite far away from the road curb and in fact, I had to sway my car so as not to run over it. As I drove past this object, I realized that it was a cat. In the past, I would have ignored the cat, happily gone home and took my rest. In any case, I was already quite tired. But on this occasion, I reacted differently. Even when I went past the cat some 20 meters down the road, I stopped the car. I sensed that the cat must have been run over by a car and she was in agony. My wife and I walked back to the cat, and indeed she was breathing heavily. I carried the cat off the road and brought her on to the pavement. As I placed her on to the pavement, she breathed her last breath. I felt such affinity to the cat; I was so glad that I was able to offer her love during her last moment. Then, a veterinarian drove past and she sensed what was happening. She stopped her car, and informed us that she had a clinic nearby. We transported the cat to her clinic, and thereafter, she took care of the body. On our way home, I said to my wife, "If not for Baba's influence, I would not have done what I did." She concurred. Is this *"Love All, Serve All"* even to a cat?

The second incident started way back in 1995 when my father-in-law left his physical body. Thereafter, my mother-in-law moved in and stayed with us. In 1996, my mother migrated from Hong Kong to Singapore but she stayed independently in a separate apartment. In the years 1999-2000, my mother went to Canada and unfortunately during that visit, she suffered a stroke, and two fractures, one in each leg. Because of her physical conditions, when she returned to Singapore in 2000, she could not stay independently anymore. Instead, she stayed in a nursing home. We felt comfortable with this arrangement because the nursing home took care of all her needs including medical needs. In fact, it would have been quite difficult for us to look after my mother at home. My wife and I were heavily loaded with our work duties. In addition, our home duties were also heavy as we had to look after three growing boys and an aging mother-in-law. Years passed and everything was fine until 2007. During that year, my mother's best friend in the nursing home suddenly passed away. My mother was badly affected emotionally and then her physical conditions, seven years after the stroke, also deteriorated. She was now a highly dependent person who required practically 24-hour assistance. The support given by the nursing home was no longer adequate; so she disliked the nursing home and demanded to come home. In view of her worsening conditions, her demand was actually reasonable and inevitable. The only problems were

(1) our home was not equipped to house a highly dependent person, and

(2) we were short-handed.

However, my mother was very stressed and depressed at the nursing home, so it was an emergency to bring her home. Just over a matter of days, we changed our sons' room to become my mother's room. We brought in furniture which was specially designed for highly dependent people. We hired a dedicated helper to look after my mother. With all these changes, our home was better equipped physically, but emotionally, we were drained. Anyway, with much trepidation, I welcomed my mother home on 5 September 2007.

With my mother staying with us, it means that there are nine of us (mother, mother-in-law, my wife and I, three sons and two maids) living under one roof, which is still happening today. Two of them (mother and mother-in-law) are approaching 100 years young. I can still remember my care free days when I was living in England on my own, when I only had to look after myself. I never imagine that I would end up with the responsibility of heading a household of nine comprising elders, youngsters, and foreign maids. To head such a household is not just challenging physically, but also emotionally. To add to the challenge, my wife and I had to handle everything single-handedly because we are an immigrant family in Singapore; so we are completely isolated. Hence, these are extremely stressful times for me and my wife. Fortunately by this time, I have already been transformed by Baba; so I see the challenge as a golden opportunity to serve. While nobody supports us physically or emotionally, Baba supports us spiritually, and with his support, I continue to serve my family to the best of my abilities. This is another of Baba's attraction – when we face challenges, he supports us. As for the two elders, I serve them with reverence, and am committed to serve them for many more years to come. Is this "*Love All, Serve All*" in action?

The third incident happened after my prostate operation in 2008. During my post-operation recovery, one evening I went for the Friday bhajans. After the bhajans, I met Brother Chandran and casually told him about the operation. Sister Savita whom we did not know before, overheard our conversation. She was interested because her husband, Brother Roopa, was also scheduled to have an operation related to the prostate. I shared my experience with them, and then found out that Brother Roopa would be having the operation at the hospital where my wife was working. At that time, I was facing challenges on three fronts:

(1) I was recovering from my third operation.
(2) I was still adjusting to my mother's home coming.
(3) I was having serious problems at work.

I called them "the three tsunamis" which hit me all around the same time. Even today, I am still feeling the effects and aftershocks of the tsunamis. Again fortunately, before the arrival of these tsunamis, I was already a transformed being. Now, I understand why Baba called me a few years earlier, so that he could prepare me for the impending tsunamis. This is another attraction of Baba – he prepares us for future challenges. So despite the challenges that I was facing, my wife and I helped Brother Roopa and Sister Savita in their hospital visits. We also visited their home which was quite far away to give them emotional support. Is this *"Help Ever, Hurt Never"* even when we are facing our own challenges?

The fourth incident happened after I started writing this book. In February 2009, I came across a talk entitled *"How to Turn a Life Experience into a Book"* by Mr. Fernando. Naturally, I attended the talk, and during the talk, I gathered that Mr.

Fernando's wife is a schizophrenic. I can empathize with him because one of my brothers is also a schizophrenic. He also informed us that he and his wife would appear on a TV programme which highlights families with mental illness patient. I sensed that the programme was important to Mr. Fernando. So on 16 March 2009 when the programme came on, I recorded it, and also made a copy on to a DVD. Subsequently, I contacted Mr. Fernando who was totally surprised because we were basically strangers; I informed him that I would like to pass him a DVD, which I did on 6 July 2009. Had I not been transformed, I doubt if I would take the troubles of recording the programme, putting it on to a DVD and then passing it to Mr. Fernando. Is this *"Love All, Serve All"* and *"Help Ever, Hurt Never"* even to a stranger?

These incidents showed the transformation in me after becoming a devotee. My behaviors toward an animal, a relative, a devotee and a stranger have all changed. I would like to think that after the transformation, I am a more humane being and a more enlightened soul. To this end, I bow at the divine lotus feet of Baba with love and humility.

Om Sai Ram!

How Sai Baba attracts without direct contact

Appendix A

Good-bad experiences

In life, we get a variety of experiences. We may consider some experiences as "good" while others as "bad". In spirituality (atmabhava), all experiences are actually considered good. Let me illustrate this with a story.

> *There was a father with two sons. This father got drunk, did not go to work, and did not look after the family. He was totally irresponsible. Then, when the elder son grew up, he also got drunk, did not go to work, and did not look after his family. He was also totally irresponsible. When people asked him why he behaved like this? He said, "With a father like mine, how do you expect me to behave?" Then, when his younger son grew up, he did not drink, he worked diligently, and looked after his family well. He was totally responsible. When people asked him why he behaved like this? He said, "With a father like mine, how do you expect me to behave?" He further elaborated that when he saw his father's behavior and how it caused pain*

> *to others, he vowed that he would behave exactly*
> *the opposite so that he would bring joy instead of*
> *pain to others.*

So, the elder son followed the "bad" behaviors, while the younger son because of the "bad" experiences actually followed the exact opposite of the "bad" behaviors. Hence, there are no "bad" experiences, only "good-bad" experiences (i.e. "bad" experiences put to good use). This is why in spirituality all experiences are considered good. For this reason, in the eyes of the Divine, everything is perfect. We can therefore learn to be good through "good" experiences or "good-bad" experiences. Either way, we become good which is the main objective of any spiritual practice (sadhana).

In Baba's discourse on 1 June 1991 entitled "*Face the Challenges of Life*", he said:

> *"What is meant by sadhana? Can japa,*
> *dhyana, bhajans and pious actions be called*
> *sadhana (spiritual effort)? Real sadhana*
> *consists in transforming bad into good ... In*
> *creation there are many things which are*
> *naturally bad. Out of these bad things, good*
> *emerges."*

Appendix B

How to become a master of life

1.0 Introduction

Are you a master or a slave of life? A simple question such as "Why do you do this?" reveals whether a person is a master or a slave of life. If the answer is "Because I have no choice," the person is a slave. For a master's answer will be "Because I choose to do it." A slave feels that he is forced to do something, therefore he has no power to choose, and is a victim of circumstance. On the other hand, a master feels that he is doing something out of choice; therefore he has freedom to choose and is empowered to do so. This difference in feeling has nothing to do with the actual happening. Both the master and the slave may be doing the same thing under the same circumstance, but one feels empowered while the other feels powerless. This article compares the beliefs of masters to those of slaves, and describes how masters live.

2.0 Master beliefs

Our feelings and actions are very much dependent on our beliefs. In order to become masters, we need to adopt the beliefs of masters. The following clarifies the beliefs of masters as compared to those of slaves.

2.1 We are spirits

Many scientific publications tell us that we are physical bodies, while many spiritual publications tell us that we are spirits. Of these two beliefs, the consequence of choosing one over the other is enormous.

Physical bodies have a beginning (birth) and an end (death). So if we choose to believe we are bodies only, we will be very concerned with the death of our bodies, because as our bodies die, so do our beings. On the other hand, if we choose to believe we are spirits, we will not be too concerned with the death of our bodies, as spirits cannot be hurt, damaged or die. As spiritual existence is guaranteed to be eternal, spiritual lives do not have beginning or end. The existence of spirits is not threatened by the death of bodies. Spirits can live with or without bodies. Hence, if we believe we are physical bodies only, we will focus on our physical lives. We will then try to keep our bodies going forever, for we do not want our beings to end. Unfortunately, physical existence is guaranteed to be temporal. No matter what we do, our bodies are destined to perish one day. We will be saddened by the death of our bodies for we believe it is also the end of our beings. Not being able to prevent the death of our bodies, we feel powerless and become slaves of life. On the other hand, if we believe we are spirits living in physical bodies, we have an added dimension – the spiritual dimension. Since spiritual lives are eternal and will definitely last much longer than physical bodies, we will focus more on our spiritual lives. We will not be saddened by the death of our bodies, and we do not do the impossible to prevent our bodies to die. Instead, we look for ways to develop our spiritual lives. As we do, we feel empowered, thereby becoming masters of life.

2.2 We are all connected

By observing our physical bodies, we see that they are separate from one another, and are not connected. So if we believe we are bodies only, we will not feel connected to our fellow beings, for your pain is not my pain. We look for differences in our bodies, and may develop the "us and them" syndrome. We may even feel hostile towards them if we perceive them as enemies or competitors. Life becomes a competition in which we have to struggle to win. So we embrace the win-lose concept, and when we win some and lose some, we feel that we are slaves of life. Moreover, are we truly winners when we take more than we need while others do not have enough?

On the other hand, if we believe we are spirits, spiritual publications tell us that we are all the same and we are connected. We may think of spirits are like air, and there is only one air covering the entire Earth. With this belief, it becomes impossible to develop the "us and them" syndrome, for your gain is my gain, and your loss is my loss. Life becomes cooperation, and we can only win if others also win. So we embrace the win-win concept, thereby becoming masters of life.

2.3 Reincarnation

If we believe we are bodies only, the issue of reincarnation does not arise because as our bodies die, so do our beings. On the other hand, if we believe we are spirits, spiritual publications tell us that as spirits, we can leave one body and subsequently take up another. If this is so, we may consider bodies are like clothes in which we wear one for one day, and change to another on another day. This belief enables us to live life without attachment to our bodies, thereby becoming masters of life.

Within reincarnation, there is one belief that by taking up different bodies, we progress in our evolution. When we evolve to a very high state, we may choose to remain as spirits forever, and there is no need to take up further bodies. However, before we reach this very high state, we are obliged to take up bodies after bodies. This belief also implies that when we live in bodies, we are at a lower state and are slaves of life. On the other hand, there is another belief that as spirits, we simply live alternately with bodies and without bodies, and this process goes on forever. With this belief, we can be at a very high state and can become masters even when we live in bodies. The latter belief is therefore more powerful. While we are in bodies, we can be masters.

2.4 We always have choice

If we believe we are physical bodies and the death of our bodies is the end of our beings, then of course we are not prepared to die. As such, we do not have the option of choosing to leave or not to leave our bodies. On the other hand, if we believe we are spirits in physical bodies, and we can take up bodies after bodies, then we always have a choice. The choice is to keep or to leave our bodies. By having such a choice, we are empowered because no one in the entire universe can then force us to do anything we do not want. Conversely, anything we do, it must be our own choosing, thereby becoming masters of life.

While we have the choice of leaving our bodies, this is of course the final choice with our present physical bodies, and we can only exercise this choice once. We should therefore exercise this choice with great wisdom bearing in mind that our bodies are sacred and we have good reasons for having them. Moreover, there are usually many other choices available to us before reaching this final choice.

More likely, we may be faced with the following. We do not wish to do certain thing but by not doing, we are afraid that we will lose certain perceived benefits. For fear of losing these benefits, we proceed to do the thing that we do not like. This in itself is not a problem. It only becomes a problem when we tell ourselves that we do not have a choice in the matter. Then, we become slaves of life. Alternatively, we can see that we have a choice. We may choose not to do that something and forego the perceived benefits (which may still happen).

Or we may decide to go ahead and do whatever so that we may reap the perceived benefits (which may not materialize). Either case, we are empowered as it is our choice, thereby becoming masters of life.

2.5 No need

By observing our bodies, we find there are many bodily needs. On the other hand, if we believe we are spirits and have the option of taking up bodies after bodies, then we do not have to be too concerned with these needs. Moreover, if we believe we are spirits, our focus is not to keep our bodies going forever. By living as spirits, we can live a life of no need because spirits do not have need. By living a life of no need, we can make our choices wisely, thereby becoming masters of life.

2.6 Great Spirit

Spiritual publications tell us that we are part of one Great Spirit, and we and the Great Spirit are one. If we believe so, whatever is good for us is good for the Great Spirit and vice versa. It is then logical to believe that the Great Spirit will only do us good, as he or she is only doing good to himself or herself. Living with such a Great Spirit, we feel empowered thereby becoming masters of life.

2.7 Cause for happening

If we believe we are physical bodies and have the physical dimension only, for any happening, we will look for physical causes only. On the other hand, if we believe we are spirits in physical bodies, then we have the added spiritual dimension. For any happening, we will look for physical as well as spiritual causes. If we believe we are one with a Great Spirit who will only do us good, we can then believe that any happening must be good for us. By adopting this belief, we feel empowered thereby becoming masters of life.

3.0 Master living

If we adopt the beliefs of masters, we may live like masters. The following discusses how the masters live with the preceding beliefs.

3.1 Spiritual living

Since the master knows that she is a spirit whose existence is eternal, she is not too interested in undertaking tasks that are merely for the sustenance of her physical body. Instead, she is much more interested to undertake tasks that are good for her spiritual being. As such, she is not too motivated by physical rewards. Instead, she is much more motivated by spiritual rewards. Her priority is to undertake spiritual tasks that enable her to know spiritual truths. By knowing these truths, a master lives with truth and discriminates against falsehood.

As the master knows that he is a spirit and not the body, he does not indulge into the pleasures of the bodily senses because he finds that spiritual inner bliss is far more enjoyable. A master also knows that when he takes up a body, life promises him nothing. A master lives a life of no expectation. Living as a spirit, the master does not have any attachment to physical objects. By having no attachment to physical objects, a master can choose not to participate in any activity, and can therefore live a life of renunciation.

3.2 Connected living

A master knows that she is connected to all others. Whatever she gives to others, she gives to herself. A master therefore lives a life of giving rather than taking. She also knows that as she serves others, she serves herself. A master therefore also lives a life of serving others. By giving and serving, a master lives a life of love and compassion. A master also knows that she is connected to humans of all races. A master therefore lives a life of racial harmony. A master knows that she is connected to nature. A master therefore lives in harmony with nature.

A master knows that if he cheats others, he cheats himself. A master therefore lives a life of sincerity, honesty and integrity. A master also knows that if he is inconsistent in his thought, word and deed, he is cheating himself and others. A master is therefore true to himself and others. A master knows what are the rights and wrongs in life. A master therefore lives a life of righteousness. A master also knows that if he attacks others, he attacks himself. A master therefore lives a life of non-violence.

3.3 Life without fear

Since the master knows that she is a spirit and can take up body after body, she is not afraid of the death of her body. By not fearing death, the master lives a life without fear. By being fearless, the master is much more prepared to undertake daring tasks that are outside her comfort zone.

3.4 Life of choosing

Since the master knows that whatever action he takes is his own choosing, his actions are empowered. Whatever he undertakes, he does with conviction, and bears the responsibility. He does not blame others for the consequence. By taking responsibility for his action, he chooses his action wisely. By accepting the consequence of his action, he is at peace with himself. A master lives a life of peace and no regret.

A master also knows that whatever action taken by others, it is their own choosing. A master therefore does not grieve when a being chooses to leave her body, as she knows it is the choice of that being.

3.5 Life of no need

Since a master lives a life of no need, he does not require anything and demands nothing. Because a master lives a life of no need, he can therefore live a selfless life and has no desire. He does not require a particular outcome to make him happy. Conversely, there is no outcome that can make him unhappy. He therefore lives a life of equanimity.

As the master lives a life of no need, she does not require any company as she does not have any social need. She also does not require any follower. A master does not have any emotional attachment. By living a life of no need, a master can choose her company wisely and she chooses good company.

3.6 Life of letting go

A master knows that he is part of one Great Spirit. Whatever task he undertakes, he knows that the Great Spirit is on his side. He therefore does what he can, and leaves the rest to the Great Spirit. A master surrenders to the Great Spirit and lets the Great Spirit determine the outcome. A master lives a life of letting go.

A master also knows that whatever she achieves, the Great Spirit is the cause and she is the instrument. A master therefore lives an egoless life.

3.7 Good life

A master knows that he and the Great Spirit are one, and the Great Spirit will only do him good. So whatever happens to him, a master knows that the Great Spirit is doing him good. A master therefore lives a good life.

4.0 Epilogue

Some of the beliefs introduced in this article may be new to you. Hence, you may be tempted to ask for proof. Let me suggest that the important issue here is not whether these beliefs are true or not, but whether they are useful in helping you to become a master of life. You may of course choose to accept and reject these beliefs. By doing so, you have actually demonstrated that you are a master of life. This is of course your true self; you may then choose to live as a master or otherwise.

4.1 Who is a master?

A master is somebody who knows the truth of beings and lives according to that truth. A master knows that she is a spirit who may live with or without a body. He also knows that the existence of the spirit is eternal, while the existence of the body is temporal. She therefore lives her life by favoring the eternal. He also knows that as a spirit, he is connected to all beings, and has no need. She therefore lives a life of detachment, honesty, love and compassion. He also knows that he is part of one Great Spirit, a master therefore lives the good life without fear and ego.

4.2 End note

A master is not somebody who has everything but someone who needs nothing. May you become a master of life!

About the author

Dr. Tommy S. W. Wong (back cover of this book) has been a spiritual seeker and a Baba follower since the end of 20th century, and became a Sai devotee at the start of 21st century. After becoming a devotee, he has given spiritual talks to various Sai groups in Singapore, and contributed spiritual articles to Sai Vahini - the annual Sai magazine of Singapore. He has also been a reader of Sai messages, a lead singer in bhajans, and a guru in the Sai Spiritual Education programme. He has visited Baba both in Puttaparthi and Whitefield, and Baba has visited him in his dreams. He is devoted to bring spiritual teachings to the world for the benefit of mankind. Further information about Dr. Wong's work can be found on his website: http://wisdomlife.page4.me/.

Printed in Great Britain
by Amazon

85280272R00064